Advance Praise

"The first thing we notice while reading C.M. Mayo is her motion, her flow, silk—line after line summoning us through story. This gift can't be manufactured. It comes from a writer, seasoned and smart, with something to say and the literary confidence to say it. I believe this is Mayo's best work—perfect words without artifice; characters and situations made permanent; a triumph of language as a natural art. She brings flowers to the living."
—Grace Cavalieri, *The Poet and the Poem from the Library of Congress*

"C.M. Mayo creates magic, in poems that transform the ordinary into something more marvelous and strange. Whether describing a haircut by the wife of "'the man who mows the lawn around the nuclear warheads,' or feuding with the neighborhood squirrels over ownership rights to nuts, or commenting on the commercialization of services in the long poem *I Will*, Mayo transforms the quotidian into something magnificent, until—as she says in the title poem—"No one would believe me/No one would believe any of this" *Meteor* is a delight and an astonishment."
—Kim Roberts, author of *A Literary Guide to Washington, D.C.*

"Whether describing a nuclear childhood of military bases with UFOs, the assassination of a hippopotamus or chaos in the hood, these poems of memory and imagination bring to life the back stories of our delirious times. To be savored."
— Bruce Berger, author of *The End of the Sherry*

"*Meteor* pierces the psyche with a dazzling presence and otherworldly light. Mayo delights in the pleasures of language and the possibilities of imagination. By leveling a playfully skeptical voice that is wholly her own, she transforms the quotidian into the outlandish while making the bizarre seem familiar and inviting. Through her inexorable wit and endless inventiveness, Mayo crafts the most unusual work—a book that is both challenging and fun to read."
—Linwood D. Rumney, judge and author of *Abandoned Earth*

Also by C. M. Mayo

Fiction

The Last Prince of the Mexican Empire
Sky Over El Nido: Stories

Nonfiction

Metaphysical Odyssey into the Mexican Revolution: Francisco I. Madero and His Secret Book, Spiritist Manual
Miraculous Air: Journey of a Thousand Miles through Baja California, the Other Mexico

Edited

Mexico: A Traveler's Literary Companion

Meteor

C. M. Mayo

Winner of the Gival Press Poetry Award

Arlington, Virginia

Copyright © 2019 by C. M. Mayo.

This is a work of fiction. Names, characters, businesses, places, events and incidents are either the products of the author's imagination or used in a fictitious manner. Any resemblance to actual persons, living or dead, or actual events is purely coincidental.

All rights reserved under International and Pan-American Copyright Conventions. Printed in the United States of America.

With the exception of brief quotations in the body of critical articles or reviews, no part of this book may be reproduced or transmitted in any form or by any means, graphic, electronic, or mechanical, including photocopying, recording, taping, or by any information storage or retrieval system, without the permission in writing from the publisher.

Published by Gival Press, an imprint of Gival Press, LLC.

For information please write:
Gival Press, LLC
P. O. Box 3812
Arlington, VA 22203
www.givalpress.com

First edition
ISBN: 978-1-940724-16-4
eISBN: 978-1-940724-17-1
Library of Congress Control Number: 2017955121

Cover art: Pantheon, Rome, Italy © 2014 Casadphoto | Dreamstime.com
Design by Ken Schellenberg.

Contents

I. Meteor
Meteor...7
Up in Michigan..9
UFO 1990...11
Man High...13

II. Davy & Me
Jade...19
Bank...20
Quite..21
Yawn...22
Zeppelin...23

III. Mango
Stay West..27
The Egg..28
Nuts...29
Mango..30
Ode To Jeff Koons....................................31
Round N Round..32

IV. In the New Territories
In the New Territories...............................35
Two Phone Calls in the Same Day......................36
En Este Pais...38
Little Bears...39
Zapata...40
From The Torre Latino Americana......................41
The Sea Is Cortés....................................43

Hippopotamus...44

IV. Silly & Serious

New...49
& Old...49
Silly..50
& Serious..50
Good...51
& Bad..51
Rich..52
& Poor...52
Clean..53
& Dirty..53
Right...54
& Wrong..54
Hors D'ouevre.......................................55
& Dessert...55
Black..56
& White...56
Silence..57
& Poem...57

VI. I Will
I Will...61

VII. The Building of Quality
The Building of Quality............................67

Acknowledgments...................................87
About the Author....................................89

To the memory of Harry Smith (1936-2012)

I. Meteor

Meteor

It's been twenty-seven years
since our toolshed was hit by a meteor
About four or five in the morning
a few days after New Year's
It sounded like a heavy door had been slammed
but none of our doors was heavy
I knew not to look at the sky
for the mushroom
the flash of white that would surely come
(My eyeballs would turn to goo
and run down my cheeks)
There was a smell of hot cement
scorched sand and grass
The dogs began to bark
our beagle Spanky
Davy Frank's cocker spaniel Mr. Murphy's poodle
The Lemmons' aged dachshund
We lived close together then
our houses all looked the same
the sidewalks were level the trees were saplings

We picked our way across the lawn
my dad had a flashlight
my mother kept her hand on my shoulder
like a vise
For the love of Lucy said Mr. Frank
He had on his work shoes
but no socks
Mr. Murphy wore a flannel bathrobe just like my Dad's
Well Walter he said
You won't need to dig a shelter now

I knew I would be famous
my photograph in the book
that told about an old man who spontaneously combusted
that showed a pumpkin the size of a Volkswagen
a girl with an extra foot growing out of her knee
But the next day
my dad brought in a truckload of dirt
> Mrs. Lemmon said she heard something about our meteor on the radio
> But she wasn't sure because she was in the shower at the time

Not long after
Apollo went to the moon
Davy Frank went to Vietnam
We moved to Dallas
The Lemmons rented an apartment by the freeway
Mr. Murphy retired to somewhere near Phoenix
last I heard
I'm sure he's dead now
Then I was transferred to Atlanta but here I am again
in a rented car
(not famous, yet)
The tree trunks are thick and craggy
the pavements cracked and buckled
most of the houses have second storeys
The children riding their bikes
all look Mexican
If I were to knock on our door
on any of these doors

No one would believe me
No one would believe any of this

Up in Michigan

For E.

I lift the nose up smooth
(the way Lindbergh would have done it)
This is a search
Nothing left to rescue
— that's for sure
The tower says Roger Foxtrot
Roger Victor
Zulu o'er hills and dales
landfills and strip malls
baseball fields and strawberry farms
Grey and brown and mud brown
the nature preserves green
so green
Four guys and their duffle bags piled into a Cessna
after a frat party
and they took off in yesterday's lightning storm
Which is amazing
— that the plane could get off the ground
We're talking body parts
This could be Ohio
could be California, near Gilroy
Grand Forks, North Dakota
Actually it's Michigan
and the cumulus are shot with crimson
The way they were last March
All those investors
had to get back to work by Monday
hail and sleet and slashing gales

The family of six and their St. Bernard
too much luggage, skis
too heavy
Up
higher than any bird will ever fly
the sky is gold
and I have nothing no dog
no sofa
No fraternity would have me
Four guys and their duffle bags piled into a Cessna
One was to be married this Saturday
The higher I go
the smaller things seem
the propeller caught in the branches of an oak tree
the tail surrounded by cows
colors strewn across the pasture

UFO 1990

Four different people who live near the Grand Forks military base
told the newspaper they saw a flying saucer
hovering above the football field
One of them is the man who mows the lawn around the nuclear warheads
(yep there is someone who does that)
His wife trims my hair once a month
Her name is Sharon
Sharon's feathering my bangs when she tells me
her brother just got back from Saudi
(yep that's what they call that place)
Sand bugs ate half his face away Sharon says
looking carefully at mine in the mirror
He woke up in his foxhole and when he touched his cheek
he felt bone
I say Yucky
because what else can you say?
Last month Sharon told me the PX was selling canned snails
But I don't know Sharon, not really
She holds the scissors point down above my scalp as she goes on
about how they gave her brother plastic surgery and then
— her scissor's blades flashing —
she tells me what they did is they took skin grafts from his thigh
Which the surgeon said can be
— she turns away and coughs into the sleeve of her shirt —
a surprisingly complex and painful process
I say Sounds like it
Sharon says You betcha
(yep that's the kind of thing they say around here)
Later when my hair is perfect
when she's pulled down the strands on each side to be sure they're even
(and they are exactly even)

I've gone back to thinking about that UFO
A snapshot of Sharon's husband is tucked into the bottom frame of her mirror
He's a heavy-set man with kind sleepy looking eyes
and a nose that looks like it's been broken
and more than once
He's wearing a UND baseball cap and squinting into the sun
as he holds up a wiener on a barbeque fork
I've seen him around
he looks like his picture
I can see him mowing the lawn around a nuclear warhead
sitting in the little bucket seat *rrrr*
steering it 'round the corner
How loud did that UFO have to be for him to look up?
Or was it
the shadow of thing
easing itself by?
I venture
Your husband is kind of famous
Sharon shrugs and says Yep
And aiming it like a gun at my ear she switches on
the blow dryer

Man High

> *The Air Force needed to know whether crew members could parachute safely from disabled aircraft flying in the stratosphere.... A young test pilot, Capt. Joseph W. Kittinger, Jr., was one of those selected to train for experiments under USAF's Project Man High... Aug. 16, 1960 was set for the ultimate test. Kittinger rode a four-and-a-half-foot open gondola to 102,800 feet...*
> — *Air Force Magazine*
>
> *The big drop is the only way home.*
> — *Captain Joseph W. Kittinger, USAF*
>   *National Geographic*

When you see our earth from an hour and a half on high
where it is a soul-chilling 94 degrees below zero Fahrenheit
you know it in your hummingbird-heart
that there are angels
gods
Because when you
        now bathed in this rawest of sunlight
        and the trumpet-blast of
silence
You who have mastered yourself
by neatly garroting every mingy cringing fear
You who (as you will tell the press) have *confidence in your team*
                confidence in your equipment
                confidence in yourself
                confidence in God
                Yea confidence in the US of A!
step off the balloon's gondola

weightless
arms splayed as if they were wings
You are one
Gazing down upon the swirled froth
that is cloud-cover
your back to the velvet canopy of blackness
and the stars
though strangely you cannot see them
they are indeed watching in their eternal sparkling silence
that knows every breath
and every intention that must form the future
You fall like a

                          knife

You have not one inch of bare skin
you are swaddled in insulation and zipped into a pressurized
suit

You must free-fall for twelve of these fourteen miles or
you will freeze
to death

Suddenly you flip and face the heavens
like a babe on his back in a crib
you are in the light but what you see is blackest night
no stars
your balloon a moth-speck of white

                          disappearing

Now you gasp for the air that is not there
no pressure
confusion
feet-first now you plunge
650 to 700 miles per hour and
Beyond
Soundlessly

Supersonic

The clouds loom up solid as a floor
but
like a spirit you pass into it
this breath inside of time
and here
like the finger of Apollo
your barometric device clicks
and your parachute blooms
open
the cage tight around your chest hauls you back

                                                                                up
where you are not welcome to stay
                    however staring your courage
                    however steeled your indifference
                    however much we all dream of it

And you float down now
strange petal
                    where the wind
shoves you
A kind of tail-less helmeted primate
wearing waffle-weave underwear
strapped into a fifty-seven pound contraption
Feeling the awful aliveness of your body
that roaring pain in your blood-swollen right hand
that strap tugging over your crotch
in your belly pushing like a brick into your lungs is
your breakfast
Orange juice and strawberry shortcake

A clearness now: the world's spectacles wiped clean:
our gray-blue world
The sweet warmth of earth pulls you

to its scarred hide
bleached with the mottle of the ancient sea's sand
> white as salt
> white as the clouds far above
> white as all the stars melted together

Thirteen minutes and forty-five seconds have elapsed since bail-out
when you hear
        the thud
of yourself
and you fall to your knees into white sand
and your chute
                      like the last silken exhalation of the heavens
falls on you
Beautiful

II. Davy & Me

Jade

We decided to rob a house
Davy & me

We wore black turtlenecks and plastic sandals
Like Vietnamese rice dealers

Our weapons were words
And an open jar of four-year-old mayonnaise

We found the lady sleeping in her curlers
In a jade green T-shirt

Davy said:
Very fine china you have, m'am

May I break a piece or two?
How about this gravy boat?

Can I use it to scratch my name into your rosewood chest?
Her face reminded me of a noise

A snattling in my glove compartment
But we didn't mean anything by it

We were just kidding
In a karmic sense

Bank

We decided to ask a lot of questions
Davy & me

Of old ladies lined up at the teller's window
Holding their purses primly

Waiting their turn
With good nature painted on their faces

Does your husband know you're here?
If we pointed a bazooka at you

How much money could you take out of your account
Right now?

They shuffled ahead
Their answers tiny as raspberry pips

Quite

We decided to act British
David & I

After cups o' cha and faggots
We purchased two black brollies

We unfurled them in the shower
The nozzle blasting cold

And read our splattered *Times*
Motionless as mummies

Yawn

We decided to leave the front door yawning open
Davy & me

The living room began to fill with swirling snow
The beagle ran out into the street

Which was a good thing
Given what we had planned next

The telephone rang and we let it *rrrr*ing and *rrrr*ing
The dog barked and barked

Spanky shut up
The neighbor yelled

Zeppelin

We decided to float
Davy & me

In a Zeppelin
With one dagger-sharp knitting needle

We were over the Mannheim soccer stadium
When Davy leaned into the silvery wall of it and said:

Shall I punch it?
The two passengers who saw this screamed

They ran to find security
Jack-knifing their arms like swastikas

Later after we'd slipped into the WC
To put on our dreadlocks wigs and Swedish clogs

We were on the observation deck
Eating Eskimo Pies

We could still remember that tiny lizard hiss
Of air

III. Mango

Stay West

> *Go west young man*
> *— John Soule*

Yesterday's tickets to Cleveland
are under a lipstick a Kleenex
a map of Seattle

and two black plastic wrapped mints
from a Japanese restaurant
where we ordered makis this and makis that

and something that squished
when you bit it
why should I go to Cleveland

there are people like you in Seattle
and with my lipstick and my map
I can find them

The Egg

The egg was very large
so I rolled it about

the carpet
down the stairs

    thlook
        thlook

and out the door
and into the street

and along the gutter
like a great big bowling ball

Mrs. Lemmon came out with her gardening shears
Where did you get that egg? she said with a *kl-snip*

I scooped it up
and tucked it under my shirt

and I ran
with it hard and cold against my ribs

Nuts

I was chased by squirrels around the block
because I stole their nuts

They are my nuts I cried
I shall make nut butters in the blender

Spread them onto banana sandwiches
with honey

Run jump into your trees
and squeak for your life

Now
when I go out to get the paper

or get into my car
Their tiny bodies are still

as plaster statues
wired to the treetrunks

and their eyes hard
as peppercorns

Mango

I was walking through an apple orchard
when a mango fell and hit me on the head
I told the people I work with about this
they laughed
A prank they said, don't be stupid
I told my friends about this
how the orchard was too far north for mangoes
how there was no one around for miles
and no one there knew my name
or my profession
or anything else about me
Finally someone I'd gone to kindergarten with
recommended an analyst
She gave me cinnamon tea and sat me on the couch
An apple orchard she said
Ah ha
and she helped me remember a painting I'd seen
of Adam in bed
surrounded by apple cores

Or were they mango pits?

Ode To Jeff Koons

Axl Rose, Arnold Schwarzenegger, Michael Jackson
How important are these people?
Not as important as J E F F K O O N S
Whenever I see a giant inflatable rabbit
whenever I see a basketball
a vacuum cleaner I think of
J E F F K O O N S

His face is flushed, his eyes shine like warming steel
That's him
fondling the blue-haired I HEART YOU trolls at JFK
J E F F   K O O N S

J E F F   knows that the naked girl in the bathtub needs to have
her head cropped
J E F F   knows that by using porcelain
we can all be King and Queen for a day
We are provincial
We need to embrace our class
(But recognize that Europe is more open)

Jeff says *I am not sophisticated*
Jeff insists I am not important

Oh no Jeff
You're the supernova of my poem

Round N Round

At the Big Sioux Truck Stop you can order a BLT
and lemme tell you
it's the best
and they give you these french fries
better than MacDonald's
you know
they're thin but juicy sort of
long and not crunchy
and you put a little ketchup on them
have a Coke
and just think
you know
after you're back out on the road
with all your tanks full
what a wonderful wonderful
oh hell

IV. In the New Territories

In the New Territories

>We pulled the Toyota to the shoulder
>tramped down the grass
>to snap a photo of
>the silver harbor water pearl horizon
>and bristling along the edge of it a steel forest
>with windows like a thousand locust eyes
>And a bird the size of my fist
>grazed your cheek cartwheeled down —
>
>If we could hear the wind singing in the pines
>It would sound like temple bells
>>iron
>>slow

Two Phone Calls in the Same Day

From Delhi A. calls to tell me
>he couldn't sleep
>for all the people crammed onto his hotel's roof
>snoring and talking and shuffling around
>at four in the morning there was screaming and snarling
>a pack of dogs fighting a troop of monkeys
>for garbage
>The people on the roof started shouting
>and throwing down stones and mangos at them
>and then everyone
>but A.
>who simply couldn't stand the heat
>went to sleep

From Palo Alto A. calls to tell me
>her neighbors were startled
>by a man in a yellow Ralph Lauren Polo shirt
>who walked in through their open front door
>When he found them drinking coffee in the kitchen
>he just coolly said hi
>so the husband thought he was a friend or colleague of his wife
>He began talking very rapidly to the husband about fly-wheels
>And so the wife thought he was a friend or colleague of her husband
>He opened the refrigerator door and helped himself to
>Cranberry juice
>Straight from the jug
>Some spilled on his shirt
>They were beginning to realize this was strange
>when from the hook by back door the man swiped the car keys
>He went into the garage
>and gunned the Mercedes

and backed out
Blam through the closed garage door

En Este Pais

A blind man cannot use a dog
in this country
even if he's rich
Or expect to receive his letters
even if they might be read to him
by a girl who can recite García Lorca
who knows the secrets of *green*
who can swim-stroke away and back again
Nothing really works
and intentions are coconut shells
full of spiders

Little Bears

The little bears clap their paws
yawn
flick their sliverthin tongues
They sniff the winter stink
Stubby waggy tails
they've yanked their tutus
up to their armpits

Breadcrusts and beer
styofoam whatnots and fruit cores
Men in overalls
ripped at the knees

The little bears do the 1-2-3
they do the cha-cha-cha
and the rumpity-pumpity *slam*

They poke their claws
through their tambourines

Zapata

On viewing David Alfaro Siquieros' "Zapata" at the Hirshorn, Washington DC

Why must he be a mask
this peasant of flesh
and heartful ambition
Why have you painted him
as a thing
Stiff
as if clay burned in a kiln
backed into it
hard against those bricks
His sombrero looks like some kind of ashtray
made of cast iron
His eyes can see
        you've shown that
But why have you given him no pupils?
His mustache is not of hair
it's a boomerang
his lip beneath it parted
in his mortal astonishment

> *Icon of pride*
> *licked with the flames of*
> *betrayal*

From The Torre Latino Americana

There was this man who wanted to jump
He'd given his wallet to the elevator boy
his car keys to the janitor
He said *Estoy cansado*
I'm tired
that's all he kept saying
Estoy cansado
He had hair the color of champagne
a double-breasted jacket
an alligator skin belt
And we wanted to help him
we really did

He kept taking in deep breaths
as if he were swallowing something enormous
and twitching one ankle
A crowd gathered below
humming humming
Somewhere in the distance there was a siren
but it was going not coming

The office manager leaned out on his elbows
Think of your children he said
and things like that
The man said please
I'm so
cansado
and he tossed out
his watch

It flashed like a small coin

and then it looked
like what it
was

The Sea Is Cortés

> *Among all these people, it was held for very certain that we came from the sky.*
> *— Alvar Nuñez Cabeza de Vaca*

An image, gorgeous as a movie still: of the explorer
ruddy-cheeked and black-bearded
Above, a sweep of ether-pure sky
A wisp of cloud floats over the horizon like a feather
The air is gentle and warm
The rigging soughs and the deckboards creak
sun-warped and dry
smelling of pitch and salt
The sails billow gently as the prow glides
over glass-smooth sea
the way yearning cuts through a life
It is so big this sea
So blue such a bright bright blue
Shield your eyes

Hippopotamus

For M., who got one

But was it one of the Big Five? he asked
He passed her the Dunhill lighter
                                                   She lit her cigar
He admired the way her cheekbones planed out
lit from below by the gleam of candlelight on the Chippendale table
                             It was a hippopotamus she said
                             She tossed the lighter back to him
                             It bounced once
                             then skimmed across the table
Where did you shoot it? he asked
                             In the river she said
He sipped his cognac
                             She lifted her glass up with her left hand
                             then swirled the cognac around the rim
                             around and around
Just in the river he said
                             Just in the river she said
Tell me about it he said
He leaned back
put one arm over the empty chair next to him
                             She said
                             It was taking a bath in the river
                             We came up in the jeep
                             and I saw its ears go like shimmy shimmy
Shimmy shimmy he said
and let out a plume of smoke
                             And so
                             She said

                          I stood up in the jeep and I shot it
How did you get it out? he asked
                          We had to wait three days she said
Why?
                          So the body could bloat up
                          Then we sent in some *Africanitos* to dive into
                          the river
                          and put a chain around it
                          Then they put the chain on a truck
                          and they pulled it
                          out
Of the river he said and he smiled
He drank some cognac
He brought his arm back around
then put both his elbows on the table and smoked
                    I'll get the hippo in about five months she said
And what will you do with it? he asked
                          I'll have frames made she said
                          She sipped her cognac
                          She puffed her cigar
                          She admired the way his cheekbones planed out
                          lit from below by the gleam of candlelight on the
                          Chippendale table
                          I'll make one little one she said
                          I'll put my picture in it
                          I'll give it to you for your birthday
Thank you he said
          You're welcome she said

IV. Silly & Serious

New

Softer than lambskin
and redder than a newborn's blood
your enormous spotted hands
that you've slathered with lotion
manicured then gloved
and kept in your pockets
all these years

& Old

Rougher than rhino hide
and whiter than a *queso fresco*
your flounder-sized feet
that you've powdered with talcum
buffed then socked
and slipped into sneakers
all these days

Silly

Flat and faded
Like the gray-green wad of bubblegum
on the underside of a cafeteria table
such a thing to come upon
that tattoo of Tony the Tiger
on your forearm
really

& Serious

Ridged and red
wound to the womb
slashed on with a horrible uncertainty
the scar from your operation for cancer
remind us
of what it reminds you

Good

Round as the holes in a flute
brilliant as polished nut shells
your indignantly flaring nostrils
perfect
for a small jewel
a silver bee

& Bad

Smoother than eelskin
and beige as a baking soda biscuit
your reconstructed nose
that you've kept in a bandage
carefully
carefully

Rich

Springier than sea sponges
and redder than Hell
your hair
My God: what's in it?
Magnolia petals
assorted confetti
your fingers

& Poor

Lighter than dryer fuzz
and brown like something sad
that sparse stringy hair on your forearms
that you really ought to shave
or cover with long sleeves
It makes my dog want to bite you

Clean

Slicker than a dolphin's flank
greyer than the driven sleet
your lips pulled tight
ears flattened to the sides of your head
as you drive my Porsche
sans windshield
Let me lend you an oblong scarf

& Dirty

Duller than lead pellets
yellow as dog piss
your teeth in a glass
going *fizzly fizzly*
although you are young
or at least maybe
not so old

Right

Sweeter than birdsong
slight like No. 2 pencils
your exquisitely delicate collarbones
that protrude from your jewel-colored blouse
happy detail of your being

& Wrong

Hard as Italian marble
obvious as a pop star
your drop-dead mah-velous torso
that you've sculpted as if it were Play-Do
that you've funneled through a T-shirt
and here you are
yes here you are

Hors D'ouevre

Tiny crispy herby
all pucker-lipped like lemons
your sweet little kiss
which I so long to nibble
but you toss it from your fingers
ta

& Dessert

Frothy as whipped cream
red like ripe raspberries
your fat smacky smooch
yum

Black

Nasty gunky
ripe as a pineapple left to fester in the summer sun
covered with a crowd of greedy flies
your *Grrrrr*owl
I cover my ears
with the innocence of two baby's bath towels

& White

Airier than gossamer
quick as a feather wafted with an updraft
the puff of your breath in winter
as you jog through a forest of pine trees
fresh
So slicingly clean
I love you

Silence

Quivery shiny sea-slug
pressed up against the roof of your mouth
Probing its cage of teeth
this muscle
it is your tongue
but you only
blink

& Poem

Etched as a vision on glass
like words in lines
and letters in words
meaning
is in the palms of your hands
show them to me

VI. I Will

I Will

Offers found on www.fiverr.com, December 10, 2010

1.

I will slice your psd into html and css
I will spy on your boyfriend
I will send you a laser cut and etched gingerbread man
    the list of zombie survival tips
    a Hot New Toy from SANTA
    a birthday card signed 'Jackie Chan' and posted from Hong Kong
    my secret blogger autoblogging technique
    my Family Secret recipe for Yummylicious Oriental
                           BBQ Chicken Wings
      a rock that I have energized with Reiki in your name
      6 origami straw stars

I will plan your wedding in an Irish castle
I will plan your trip to Singapore
I will answer 10 questions about Berlin, Germany
    4 make-up and beauty questions
    three surveys of your choosing
    2 questions about being a Pilot
    a Contact Lens question

                Any question you have about the Navy
                Anything you need to know about frogs

    I will ask my Magic 8 Ball any question for you

2.

I will tell you my honest opinnion [sic] about a book your [sic] writing
I will proofread your essay and correct it with feedback too!
I will revise your resume
I will review your French resume
I will read a poem to you really well
I will read the headline of your choosing while in a man-sized chicken suit
    I will write a short, cheesy rap about the topic of your choice
                      and perform it on video dressed as a hotdog

I will record your Christmas message in my beautiful British accent
    yell any English word or sentence out of my third story window
        and record it with my webcam
    sing and record song in russian for u
    listen to your own song and tell you what I think about it
    listen to that secret you carry around with you
    listen to you vent and rant about anything under the sun for 20 minutes
        for 10 minutes. Vent, rant, opine, bounce ideas, cry, whatever

    I will listen to you complain about fibromyalgia

3.

I will do anything from Los Angeles
        create a blogspot blog for you
        make it snow on your blog!
        integrate the facebook connect in your blog
        promote your tumblr on my quite popular tumblr

I will inform you about Pakistan
I will tell you the true story of Santa Claus
I will teach you how to make a ball of fire in your hand
        Java programming for half an hour

I will check your Japanese tattoo to be sure it says what you think it says

I will turn anyone into a stamp
    remove scars and enhance 3 of your photos
    take a photo of anything you want in San Francisco
    mail a random, anonymous, hand-drawn sketch to anyone of your choosing
    give you joomla template unique design
    tweet to 17,000 followers twice
    show You How To Remove Thesis link Attribution at the
        bottom of the Thesis Theme

    I will have my dog eat a copy of your homework

I will call your child as Cookie the Elf and record it for you
I will write your child a letter from Kermit the Frog
I will write a 5 page Fairy story in your child's name
I will write a phrase of your choice on my body
I will write your name or business on my arm or back
    and walk around St Louis for a day
I will write your name in Sharpie on the side window
    of my awesome old station wagon

I will write your name on a grain of rice

4.

I will create and say a prayer for you or a loved one for 30 days
                              and then release it to the universe
I will say a deep prayer for you for 10 minutes
I will write 7 personalized prayers for you regarding any situation
I will pray for you every night for 5 nights
I will pray to Jesus for you for 3 days
I will say the Rosary for you on 2 consecutive days

I will say a prayer for you and donate the money to my church

> I will send your prayer requests to the throne of God
> I will tie your deepest wish to a live tree

I will be your penpal and send you cute stuff!

I will play duke nukem 3D on xbox live
I will teach you the basics of the secret language Double-Dutch
I will send your Jewish friends a letter from Santa
> your child a letter from Santas reindeer, Rudolph
> your songs to Radio station in London England, UK
> you a set of my custom bat house plans
>> an authentic solid silver US Mercury dime
>> the best recipe for baked ZITI ever
>> 1 handcrafted tuxedo fish ornament if you live in the US or Canada

5.

I will do absolutely nothing
I will accept a tip or bonus
> humbly accept a tip
> begrudgingly accept gratuities if you must

I will accept your donation
I will accept your $5 and be very grateful for $5

VII. The Building of Quality

The Building of Quality

> *The average citizen — who went to school in a building modeled on a shoe factory, who works in a suburban office park, who lives in a raised ranch house, who vacations in Las Vegas — would not recognize a building of quality if a tornado dropped it in his yard.*
> *— James Howard Kunstler, The Geography of Nowhere*

I.

The deadness in the air
The obscene smell of torn earth
In the Smiths' front yard the oak had heaved over
its roots like hag's hair scraggled across the sidewalk
The lamp post had been snapped in half like a pencil
Glass sparkled on the asphalt of the driveway
and a green tricycle had launched itself into what was left of the elm
and the lid of
— was that a washing machine?
Shit John said Shit. Shit
He clenched shut his eyes, and when he opened them again he said
Shit
His wife Jane clutched at her bathrobe
She felt sick — exactly the way she had that ghastly day
eleven years ago when she was fired as the hostess at the Red Lobster
out by the Wal-Mart and not for anything she'd done or not done
or said or even dared to consider —
it had come smack out of the blue: the wrath of Bob Haskins
Jane bit her lip so hard it bled
And then she swallowed

You check the backyard she said to John because she'd grabbed the phone
which unlike their wide-screen Sony TV was still in the wall
9-1-1 she punched the numbers with her thumb
then on hold she drummed her fingernails against the Formica
just as lickety-split as she could type in data
(patient records for the ABC Medical Group)
John who — strange is fate — had Bob Haskins' job
managing what was now a Pizza Hut
and no matter how he might yell at the kids who
sloppily slapped the dough around and forgot to mop up the men's room
always
numbly
did as he was told
pushed open the screen door
It flew off its hinge and into — *klelk-k* —
the Parkers' legless ping pong table
Jane slammed down the phone and came running
What she saw from the back door was
their $3,659 deck smashed into matchsticks
scattered all down the hill to the highway
The hedge had been blown away
and now they could see the cars speeding by
tiny and bright as pellets of chewing gum *zoom zoom*
as if the terror they had suffered had never happened *zoom*
or ever would happen again ever
Zoom
Under the razor-sharp sky was this:
Shining droning indifference

II.

Jane slapped herself on the cheek — What in thundernation?
She gasped because there — at the bottom of their backyard
where the gas grill they'd bought at Home Depot for $499 had been parked
— was a building!
Could that maybe be some class of toolshed? She wondered
John said Looks kinda like a kids' playhouse
Jane said Or a muffin (because of its dome)
It had an egg-shaped window over its door
and a window on either side so that the front seemed a face staring back
at them with a most peculiarly perplexing question
John scratched at the back of his neck and said Dunno
(He had a kind of creepy feeling about it)
He said to Jane as if she were privy to some secret
and undoubtedly feminine knowledge that he was not:
Anybody in there?
Making her hands into a bullhorn Jane called out Yoo hoooo!
In the far distance (past the Parker's house) there came back the tinny sound
— woven in with the highway's —
of the Delanos' Rottweiler frantically barking.
Jane marched down the slope and rapped the door with her knuckle
Solid she said
You go in first
John did as he was told
The interior was the white of pastry cream
On its floor it had tiles laid out in checkerboard
the black ones shined like onyx mirrors
Above rose the dome dove-gray and suffused with a mysterious and delicate light
The floor space was too small to dance in but large enough for a sofa
— not that it had one
Standing in the middle of it John clapped and it echoed: *(clap)*
Clap!

     (clap)
Clap!
     (clap)
Cut it out it will you? Jane said
and then touching the door's hinge: The fixtures they're kinda old timey
Its walls were bare but for a drawer built into one side
The knob was shaped like a frog and Jane wondered could it be solid brass?
John tried to unscrew it but it was stuck
Inside the drawer — Jane leaned down and felt around —
there was only a stain shaped like a pig that looked like
a spill of Coca-Cola
Then John noticed the mahogany moldings
all carved with acanthus leaves and roses
He said Wiggy
which was something he'd picked up from the kids at Pizza Hut
Other than a little dust a few acorns and leaves
and a spider curled up dead in the corner
the whole of it was as clean as a baby's soul
Shit John said and he pointed out the window at their own house
The vinyl siding — the vinyl siding that had cost them $1,850
and that they'd been paying off for $69.99 a month
since last January —
had been shorn clean off
Jane she couldn't help it she burst into tears
Hold me she said
John held her

III.

The wonderful thing about this peculiar little muffin of a building
— and already in the three days it had sat in their back yard
the Smiths had come to think of it as "theirs"—
was that it made them forget every now and then for a few minutes
the heartbreak of all they had lost:
$3,659 hardwood deck
$999 wide-screen Sony TV
$399 a month Chevy SUV
$299 ping pong table (completely blown away; that legless one in the
backyard belonged to the Parkers)
$499 gas grill (nowhere to be seen)
$1,859 vinyl siding
screen door busted off its hinges
the hedges
the elm
that leafy old oak the squirrels used to make their nests in
The insurance-claim list (Jane had typed it) went on for three pages
single-spaced
You forgot the lawn stuff the deer and the light-up elf John said
when he read it and at that
Jane dropped her head in her hands
When the insurance man put everything back into his briefcase he said
Our Lord was looking out for you two
The way it's constructed you're lucky as spit
your house is still on its foundation
His crew-cut was like brush-bristles
He clipped his pen into the pocket of his shirt and turned to the door to go
— but Jane wanted to know:
Who's going to pay to have that building in the backyard hauled outta here?
The insurance man
keeping his hand on the doorknob
twisted his mouth
That's the oh ten thousand dollar question I'd say

First someone's got to claim it, don't they?
John chuckled
Here little building he said
Here little building
The insurance man kept a straight face
I've seen stranger he said
Delanos down your block?
There's a Safeway shopping cart in their swimming pool
Wiggy John said because the Safeway was six miles clear
on the other side of the highway
Jane said nothing because she knew
Patty Parker had swiped that Safeway cart
six months ago and kept it in her side yard by the trash cans
Well said the insurance man already a foot down the front steps
It's like Our Lord puts His world in the blender
and every once in a while
He lets Satan push the button
Whatever Jane said rudely
(She hated it when people started up with this fire and brimstone stuff)
I want that building off of our property and I don't want to pay
one red cent for it
Just thinking about it her throat felt tight
Just thinking about it John felt a clenched fist in his gut
They watched the insurance man's red Honda disappear down the street
Then they micro-waved some White-Castle hamburgers and
because the TV was busted
they drove out to the mall to see a movie starring Julia Roberts

IV.

The next day the neighbors came to see the little building in the backyard
They had their own troubles mostly they talked about those
Shelly Farmer allowed that the building was kind of pretty
Rudy Delano (he was one of those who left his dog chained up in the sun
and just let it bark all day) crossed his arms and said Seriously weird
It's a tomb or something didya check that drawer for ashes?
He left muddy boot-prints all criss-crossed in a mess
The day after that Jane faxed a press release
but there was no spot on local TV
They put flyers up all along Route 3
Weeks went by
Jane called the insurance man
his secretary said he was on vacation in Las Vegas
Patty Parker came by to borrow a cup of Crisco
She said Why doncha try selling it
to that miniature golf course out on the highway?
And by the way you know it was your screen door
that laid that scratch into our ping pong table
We got the legs back on but whenever the ball hits that scratch
it bounces funny
She flapped her hand —
like, *bling!*
Ah *feel* ya pain John said in his best Bill Clinton drawl
and then he laughed and went on channel surfing
on his new wide-screen Panasonic TV
When the insurance man came back from vacation
he did not return Jane's calls
Out of spite she considered telling John to just tear it down
But would that even be possible? She wondered
The little building seemed to be made of something as solid and sober as the moon
it looked bluish in the dawn
and then with the early sun tinged gold

as if it might be warm to the touch
Zoom the sun seemed to rise with the sounds of the cars racing by
on the highway
zoom zoom higher into the sky
and just before Jane had to leave for work
from the back door she could see
the little building's big-shouldered shadow begin to pull into itself
(Inside with the door shut, you could hear nothing
but your own breathing and the rush
of your own heart)
As for their own two-story split-level ranch-style tract house
nails went into the walls easy as thumbtacks
The doors swung out light as feathers
pm-m-m into their Home Depot rubber stoppers
The plasterboard walls were so thin that in the den
you could hear whatever embarrassing thing was going on in the bathroom
and in the bathroom
you could hear someone talking on the phone in the kitchen
The kitchen counters were the ones the builder put in
a yucky avocado-green already streaked and pocked with burn marks
The air conditioning unit hung out of the front bedroom
like the back end of a jack-ass said Doug
But what did Doug know?
Doug was Jane's little brother
a Fed Ex truck driver who lived in Florida in a sweaty little condo
that looked like a shoe factory
Doug called their house a *McMansion*
Obviously
he was just jealous

V.

Somehow her little building — the way it was so different? —
reminded Jane of England
where her Grandma Tuttle had taken her the summer after high school
Though it was not at all like the buildings she took pictures of there
Such as Shakespeare's thatch-roofed house
From behind the rope she had peered into his dim little bedroom and
marveled at how low its ceiling was
the timbered walls so primitive
In the gift shop Grandma Tuttle bought her a T-shirt
with a swan on it
and four postcards she forgot to send
They'd been herded through Blenheim too
beneath its soaring ceilings
crisp ice-pale blues and baby pinks
everything huger than a dream and NO TOUCHING fine
A few years ago in *People* magazine
she'd read that Sylvester Stallone got married there
Jane admired Sylvester because
her own secret daydream was to be
a screenwriter
Years ago when she was working as the hostess at Red Lobster
she had gotten this idea for a screenplay
It was based on a true story
(and aren't those the ones that always sell?)
A meteor had landed on their neighbor's toolshed at four in the morning
just three days after New Year's
It sounded like a truck had slammed into a brick wall
The dogs began to bark —
Davy Frank's cocker spaniel
Mr. Murphy's poodle
the Lemmon's arthritic and half-deaf dachshund
(though not her own cockapoodle Spot
who had cowered moaning and trembling like a Jell-O

beneath the blankets)
What had happened to everyone afterwards? That was her idea
Where did Mr. Lemmon go after he bought that power boat and
— just as Mom predicted — dumped his wife Thelma for Mrs. Murphy?
Arizona?
Oregon?
Davy Frank died in the '68 Tet Offensive
both legs blown off at the hips
It was true he had teased poor Spot with his Hula-Hoop
and once he tried to make Doug (who was eleven)
shoplift an Eskimo Pie
Still (secretly) Jane had a crush on Davy
She'd never written her screenplay
But these many years later
married to John Smith
who was fading to gray at the temples
getting a gut as the manager of the Pizza Hut
Jane often found herself thinking of Davy
his James Dean hair
his slack nasty smile
that even then seemed to know the evil that would be his fate
And now in the half hour after work and before sundown
(when she used to watch TV)
she would go into her little building alone to sit on the floor
to just think
do some breathing exercises
It seemed to her sometimes that his spirit
a vague coldness
was hovering behind her shoulder whispering something
— something she tried but could not
quite
understand

VI.

After three months had passed and no one had claimed their building
John continued to mow around it
Jane said they might consider putting up trellises on its sides
for tiny roses
wouldn't that look nice?
John thought he might use the building for an art studio
but what he said was
they should use it to store all that crap they had in the garage
Make more room for the cars
Let him set up a couple of saw-horses and a plank
Work with his power-tools
Jane said But it could be a guest room for Doug
Nah John said
Doug'll just hafta be a fancypants and sleep in our
McMansion
That made Jane chuckle
He used his electric drill to nail up the trellises
And then one Sunday when Jane was out at the mall
he hauled in from the garage
those boxes of old clothes and textbooks
and broken answering machines
and dead radios
and that Veg-O-Matic gizmo Doug gave them for their wedding
that never worked
and some of the rusted lawn furniture too
which scratched hell into the tiles on the floor
Seeing it all piled in there
John wiped his brow on his sleeve and laughed at himself
Art Studio?
Whatever had made him think he was *artistically inclined?*
True he used to be able to play "The House of the Rising Sun"
on the electric guitar
But there was something wrong with its wiring and one day

— he was in Davy Frank's garage practicing chords —
it gave him such a ghastly shock
it singed the pads of his fingers
He didn't feel right after that for about three days
Heavy was what Davy said
Had he been alive today he would have said
You suck
When John was little his Mom liked to ask him
What do you want to be when you grow up?
His brother Joe wanted to be a pilot
(and ended up in jail for dealing dope)
His sister Jill said she would be the bestest nurse
(and ended up an anesthesiologist who drives a Lexus)
John said
— because he was only five and
he really liked playing with his Play-Do —
he wanted to be a sculptor!
Hah Mom said
Being an artist that's no way to feed a family
From the depths of his Lay-Z-Boy Dad said
What
is my son some of kind of poof?
OK fireman John said I wanna be a fireman!
That's nice Mom said
Though John did not want to be a fireman
He thought they looked dumb in that stupid bucket of a helmet
Who would want to have to lug around a hose that looks like a python?
And risk getting burned or killed
Or wet
Always tired
And so after graduating from the local state college with a perfect C average
he ended up managing the Pizza Hut that used to be the Red Lobster
married to the girl
— so beautiful she was then —
who got fired by Bob Haskins

VII.

For their fifteenth anniversary John wanted to go to Las Vegas
The travel agency had a package: 4 days, 3 nights, $599
They could see the Cirque du Soleil
and those two German dudes with their albino tiger
But Jane had decided that since they'd had their honeymoon in Disneyland
they would visit the other coast: Washington DC
John liked the Air & Space Museum best
He didn't want to go to the Vietnam Memorial but Jane insisted
It was hot enough to melt plastic and muggy
He had a blister on his heel
Compared to the heft of the Lincoln Monument
the cool spear of the Washington Monument, and there in the hazy distance
the imperial dome of the Capitol
the Vietnam Memorial was
— John said what he'd read somewhere —
a gash of shame
It was bug-ugly Jane agreed
But curious the way the black stone shone like a mirror
She watched herself walking down the path
drawn along as if into the belly of the earth itself
and John behind her
a silhouette of a baseball cap
When she started to read all the names she began to cry
(How would she ever find Davy Frank's?)
She didn't have the words for what she felt only
a blunt sense of dread and loss
She remembered how Mrs. Frank's face looked on the day after
she got her telegram
The Beetles on the radio so obscenely sunny bopping *yeah yeah yeah*
The insects' sneering rattle unseen in the trees
She wanted to ask someone for help
there were so many people all round-bottomed and round-bellied

drinking bottled water
It was like at Disneyland but here
no one was smiling and it was as quiet
— other than the presidential helicopter that *whoozzzed* overhead —
as a church
Afterwards they walked along the reflecting pond and then through trees to
another pond that mirrored a unusually solid-looking muffin-shaped cloud
and suddenly Jane thought of the gardens at Blenheim
the reflecting pools like these so grand and pea-green delicate
the willow tree
the geese
a sound — where was it coming from? — of trickling water

VIII.

Five years later Bob Haskins
who had been in jail for assaulting his ex-wife with a claw hammer
was back in town
He sauntered into Pizza Hut and ordered a LARGE
with onions and bell-peppers and three meats
and when he took out his wallet to pay
he sank to the floor
dead
of a massive heart attack
There was a strangely satisfying kind of closure in this
Jane told Doug when she phoned him in Florida
And it was a good example for John because he started to watch his weight
jog
eat more broccoli and fish
She called Salvation Army
and from the building out back
had them haul away the boxes of old clothes and text books
all that rusted lawn furniture
(The leg of the chaise left a gouge in the door
that Jane fixed with a brown Magic Marker)
Jane had grown so fond of their little building
the way it was bloomed over with climbing peppermint-pink roses
every spring
And now that it was cleared out again
and she'd mopped the scratched and stained floor
so she could sit on it
she sat on it
Indian-style with her hands palm-up on each knee
She raised her face to the light of its little dome closed her eyes
and filled her lungs and she heard in her mind
the voice of Julia Roberts
It's been twenty seven years

since our toolshed was hit by a meteor...
She had an urge to rush to the computer and start typing but instead
she smiled
and stayed
doing her breathing exercises

IX.

They were both sixty-five when they decided to take their pensions
and move to Florida to be near Doug and his kids
There was no one else left
When they put their house on the market the real estate agent breezed
through each room until throwing open the back screen door
she said:
What in thundernation —?
She had not known about the tornado
(she'd moved here from Chicago only six years ago)
Her name was Leeza Linsey and she featured herself prominently in her
ads
Leeza Linsey's words came at them like punches:
Zoning doesn't allow this
Violation of building codes
I can't sell this property if you don't remove it
Their insurance company had been merged
with another insurance company
which had been taken over in a leveraged buyout
by a German venture capital fund
and then merged with an offshore subsidiary
of a financial conglomerate based in Japan
(or maybe it was the Netherlands)
It's name was something completely different now
the records were all in a warehouse in deepest
New Jersey
And so
in the end
the Smiths had to pay to have it hauled away
Jane paid the bill and when she ripped the check out of her checkbook
she said: There goes our Las Vegas vacation
Shit John said Shit shit
He clenched shut his eyes, and when he opened them again he said
Shit

The demolition company sent a couple of Mexicans in hardhats
They had to use a wrecking ball
and a jackhammer to break up the floor
All day long the dogs barked
the poodle next door
the three-legged spaniel
Patty Parker's arthritic and mange-addled afghan *rufruf rrrruf!*
Neither Jane nor John knew the dogs' names anymore
When it was gone their lawn had a gigantic bald spot
Our very own crop circle John said
Jane elbowed him in the stomach
They both laughed
But then Jane cried
She cried for her pretty little muffin house
and her friends at the ABC medical group
She cried for Route 3
and the oak
— the new oak —
the way it would look in the fall gold
as if covered with coins
In Florida she would never see any of them again
Hold me she said
John held her
Then because Jane told him to
John drove out to the Wal-Mart for grass seeds and a bag of fertilizer
On the way home even though he wasn't hungry
he wolfed down a Whopper with bacon and cheese
He stopped at the mall to throw out the bag
and the balled up wrapper
so Jane wouldn't find them

X.

In Florida Doug's kids told all their friends
about Aunt Jane and Uncle John's muffin house
And then a few years later they told their own children and to prove it
showed them the yellowed pictures in Aunt Jane's photo album
which she had left in their house when
because of her Alzheimer's John put her into the nursing home
A generation later
when one branch of the family told the story
the little building became the neighbor's swimming pool cabaña
In another more distant branch
a gazebo
Most couldn't care less
The past for them had been shorn away
It was moldy old school stuff
facts and dates like bitter Vitamin pills to be swallowed
'Cuz
None of them knew
— Jane Smith herself did not know —
that they were the direct descendants of the elder brother
of Lieutenant Colonel Jared O'Higgins
a poet of the Appalachians who played his own ballads
on a dulcimer he had made with his own hands
Slender girlish hands:
he held in them a telegram for General William Tecumseh Sherman
and because it was urgent he came running
his boots kicking back dust
Ahead of him the General's tent waited wedding white
it billowed and shuddered in the spring breeze
And just as the General himself came out
his blue coat hanging open
a cigar in his hand
a cannonball blew Jared O'Higgins' head off clean at the neck
His body

— just before it collapsed —
kneeled on the dirt before the General
It was such a sight to see so strange
The aide-de-camp staring down at the boy's body
(its blood had spurted onto the side of the tent
and was pooling blackly into the earth)
crossed himself violently
The General clenched his jaw so hard
it gave him a headache for the next three days
But he was a hard-bitten warrior
who had already paddled every inch of war's river of grisliness
its cruelty and its stupidity
which are really the same thing
It was an accident: no Rebel was anywhere nearby
No one told the *Washington Star* reporter who was there that day
The General said nothing about it in his memoirs

XI.

Sharon Uwefu Wallis was the great great great great great niece
who ended up with Jane Smith's peeling and brittle photo album
She treasured it but when she moved to London
out in the middle of the calm Atlantic
the container it was packed in was swept
by a freak wave
overboard
From the insurance company Sharon received a substantial settlement:
enough to scour London's antique shops for whatever she wanted
and decorator upholstery to boot
But for my antique photos?
She had aimed her voice at the SVM (satellite-video monitor)
The insurance agent
(whose office was in one of those sprawling office parks on the moon)
kindly reminded her that the contract did not cover
articles of a personal nature
that had not been professionally appraised
The agent's name was Richard Haskins and yes
he was a direct descendent of Robert "Bob" Haskins the serial killer
who (it was discovered after his death from a heart attack in a Pizza Hut)
had buried 13 women including his neighbor Thelma Lemmon
and her dachshund
in the crawl-space beneath his back porch
That was a helluva wave Richard Haskins
said too loudly into the SVM
If you'll excuse my French
You're lucky the whole enchilada didn't buy the farm
Am I? Sharon said rudely
(She hated it when people attempted to manipulate her with fatuous
and needlessly clashing clichés)

Soon afterwards
one day over tea with scones (and the most delicious clotted cream)
Sharon told her new friends about the freak wave
out in the middle of the perfectly calm Atlantic
that had washed overboard all of her living room furniture
and a box that contained her great great great great great aunt's photograph
of a most eccentric little domed building she'd had in her garden
It looked like a popover
It had always seemed to her so incongruously exquisite
a sort of architectural folly
a Masonic pavilion?
Or perhaps a personal library *sans* shelves
Whatever it was
a tornado had dropped it in their garden
fully intact
Oh you Americans Fiona Witherspoon said
and she clucked her tongue
A likely bit of poetry!

Acknowledgments

BorderSenses: "Man High"
Exquisite Corpse: "Egg"; "Nuts"
Gargoyle: "UFO, 1990"
Good Foote: "Good & Bad"
The Green Tricycle: "In the New Territories"
The Kenyon Review: "The Building of Quality" (as a short story)
Lyric: "Clean & Dirty"; "Rich & Poor"
The Mexico City News: "Stay West"
Muse Apprentice Guild: "Ode to Jeff Koons"; "Silence & Poem"
Natural Bridge: "Up in Michigan"
Permafrost: "From the Torre Latinoamericana"
The Quarterly: "Hippopotamus"
Saint Ann's Review: "Two Phone Calls in the Same Day"; "En Este País"
Rio Grande Review: "Mango"; "Nafta"
West Branch: "Little Bears"
Witness: "Bank"; "Jade" (both in "Crime in America" issue); "Zapata" ("Ethnic America" issue)

"Meteor" was published in the anthology edited by Andrei Codrescu and Laura Rosenthal, *American Poets Say Goodbye to the Twentieth Century*, Four Walls Eight Windows Press, 1996, and the anthology edited by Virgil Suárez and Ryan van Cleave, *Red, White & Blues*, University of Iowa Press, 2004

"Right & Wrong" was published in the anthology edited by John B. Lee, *Body Language: A Head-to-Toe Anthology*, Black Moss Press, Canada, 2003

"The Sea is Cortés" was both displayed and published in a bilingual version (Spanish translations by Luis Alberto Ambroggio) in *Our Voices, Our Images: A Celebration of Hispanic Heritage Month*, Inter-American

Development Bank Cultural Center, August 18-October 17, 2003

I would like to most gratefully acknowledge poet and essayist Harry Smith (1936-2012), who was a close friend of my father's, for his encouragement and the inspiration of his example. He was wildly creative, courageous, generous, and kind.

I also have many more poets and writers to thank for reading and commenting on these works over the years—so many years that I cannot trust my memory to bring every name to mind. If I have forgotten you, please know that all the same, bodacious karma prevails! Mary Azoy, Consuelo de Aerenlund, Kate Blackwell, Jennifer Clement, Brandel France de Bravo, Judith Infante, Martha Black Jordan, Margaret Kelly, Ann L. McLaughlin, Leslie Pietrzyk, Manuel Ulacia, and Mary Kay Zuravleff.

A bouquet of thankyous to Linwood D. Rumney, for selecting this manuscript for the Gival Press Poetry Award.

At Gival Press, my very warmest appreciation to editor Robert L. Giron, and to Ken Schellenberg for the cover design. It can be a lonely road to publication and it means the world and the moon and all the planets to me to "link arms" and skip along with you!

Finally, for the great gifts of residencies over the years, I thank the MacDowell Colony, Ragdale Foundation, Virginia Center for the Creative Arts, and Yaddo.

About the Author

C.M. Mayo has published poetry and fiction in many literary magazines, among them, *Beltway Quarterly, Bordersenses, Gargoyle, Rio Grande Review, Saint Ann's Review, Kenyon Review, Paris Review,* and *Southwest Review,* and in numerous anthologies including those edited by Robert L. Giron, *Poetic Voices Without Borders* and *Poetic Voices Without Borders 2.* Mayo's works of fiction include the novel *The Last Prince of the Mexican Empire,* a *Library Journal* Best Book and the short story collection *Sky Over El Nido,* which won the Flannery O'Connor Award; her nonfiction books include *Metaphysical Odyssey into the Mexican Revolution: Francisco I. Madeo and His Secret Book, Spiritist Manual*; and *Miraculous Air: Journey of a Thousand Miles through Baja California, the Other Mexico.* She is also a noted translator of contemporary Mexican poetry and fiction and is the editor of *Mexico: A Traveler's Literary Companion.* A native of El Paso, Texas, she was raised in California, educated at the University of Chicago, and has been a long-time resident of Mexico City. In 2017 she was inducted into the Texas Institute of Letters. Visit her website: *www.cmmayo.com*

Poetry from Gival Presss

12: Sonnets for the Zodiac by John Gosslee

Abandoned Earth by Linwood D. Rumney

Adama: Poème / Adama: Poem by Céline Zins with English translation by Peter Schulman

Bones Washed in Wine: Flint Shards from Sussex and *Bliss* by Jeff Mann

Box of Blue Horses by Lisa Graley

Camciones para una sola cuerda / Songs for a Single String by Jesús Gardea with English translation by Robert L. Giron

Dervish by Gerard Wozek

The Great Canopy by Paula Goldman

Grip by Yvette Neisser Moreno

Haint by Teri Ellen Cross Davis

Honey by Richard Carr

Let Orpheus Take Your Hand by George Klawitter

Metamorphosis of the Serpent God by Robert L. Giron

Meteor by C. M. Mayo

Museum of False Starts by Chip Livingston

On the Altar of Greece by Donna J. Gelagotis Lee

On the Tongue by Jeff Mann

The Nature Sonnets by Jill Williams

The Origin of the Milky Way by Barbara Louise Ungar

Poetic Voices Without Borders edited by Robert L. Giron

Poetic Voices Without Borders 2 edited by Robert L. Giron

Prosody in England and Elsewhere: A Comparative Approach by Leonardo Malcovati

Protection by Gregg Shapiro

Psaltery and Serpentines by Cecilia Martínez-Gil

Refugee by Vladimir Levchev

The Silent Art by Clifford Bernier

Some Wonder by Eric Nelson

Songs for the Spirit by Robert L. Giron

Sweet to Burn by Beverly Burch

Tickets for a Closing Play by Janet I. Buck

Voyeur by Rich Murphy

We Deserve the Gods We Ask For by Seth Brady Tucker

Where a Poet Ought Not / Où c'qui faut pas by G. Tod Slone

For a complete list of Gival Press titles, visit: *www.givalpress.com*.

Books available from Follett, Ingram, Brodart, your favorite bookstore, on-line booksellers, or directly from Gival Press.

Gival Press, LLC
PO Box 3812
Arlington, VA 22203
givalpress@yahoo.com
703.351.0079

www.ingramcontent.com/pod-product-compliance
Lightning Source LLC
Chambersburg PA
CBHW020946090426
42736CB00010B/1282